Science Technology Engineering Maths
STEM STARTERS FOR KIDS

ROBOTICS
ACTIVITY
Book

Written by Jenny Jacoby
Science education consultant : Dr Sue Dale Tunnicliffe

Designed and illustrated by
Vicky Barker

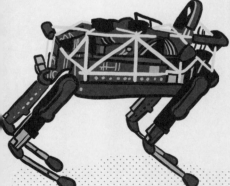

www.bsmall.co.uk

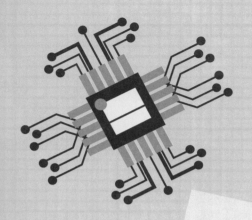

Published by
b small publishing ltd.

www.bsmall.co.uk

· 1 2 3 4 5 ·

Production by Madeleine Ehm
Design and art direction by Vicky Barker
Science education consultant: Dr Sue Dale Tunnicliffe
Printed in China by WKT Co. Ltd.

British Library
Cataloguing-in-
Publication Data.

A catalogue record for this
book is available from the
British Library.

ISBN
978-1-912909-07-0

WHAT IS ROBOTICS?

Robotics is the designing and building of robots by engineers to meet a need identified by someone such as a scientist or another engineer. Robots are powered machines with a particular job to do. Humans enter code into the robot's program, which leads the robot to perform an action.

WHAT IS STEM?

STEM stands for 'science, technology, engineering and mathematics'. Engineers can use these four areas to come up with ways to design and build robots. Robots can also do jobs to help us investigate science more deeply by helping do the engineering jobs and mathematical calculations that are too difficult for one human mind!

Science

Technology

Engineering

Maths

WHAT MAKES A ROBOT?

A robot is a machine that works automatically, and that adapts to feedback – which means that it can tell when its job is done or if its surroundings have changed.

Robots need four things:

A JOB TO DO
– most robots are designed to do just one job or one series of jobs

SENSORS
– some way to tell what is happening in its environment

A 'BODY'
– to respond to what the sensors are telling it

POWER
– batteries, or plugged into an electricity source

TRUE OR FALSE

Circle the statements that are true about robots, and cross out those that are false. Check your answers on page 30.

ROBOTS CAN PLAY CHESS

ROBOTS ARE ALWAYS MADE OF METAL

ROBOTS CAN DANCE

ROBOTS ARE USED TO DIFFUSE BOMBS

ROBOTS HAVE TWO ARMS AND TWO LEGS

MICROSCOPIC ROBOTS CAN TRAVEL AROUND YOUR BODY TO CURE DISEASE

ROBOT DESIGN

When designing a robot, engineers need to consider four things:

IDEA
The starting point: what job will the robot do?

MECHANICS
This is the physical way the robot moves – if it will move, how?

ELECTRONICS
The electronic parts of the robot and how they will be powered.

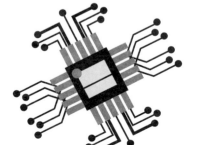

PROGRAMMING
Programming the right instructions so the robot can do its job.

Can you find these robotic words in this word search?
Words can read backwards, forwards, up, down and diagonally.

```
d t h j d e l q s x y d e o h v p
y o n u p n t c r i l q g i u v e
k t i y t a s k u s e d i n e n a
c g d k c r u s l e e h w x g n n
a a e o c m i t o d a a e i r t u
b n a i g x e o u s t h s i t l t
d f s y j l t t e s v e h l f e a
e y w g o e u n c t d p l m v u i
e c v x s g s e r y i n e e o h l
f r s r i o p e s l o v u c l n p
h e t u r c v i o g l r u h c e o
i h p r o g r a m m i n g a r t w
c t j u r b c k s t i w n n n l e
d s y i s y f d s z h a a i o u r
a y i v o l c u j a m g o c e y c
s e l e c t r o n i c s c s i k j
g e t c u z y s e o j a v t f v a
```

programming **sensor** **task**

mechanics **electronics** **design**

ideas **power**

wheels **feedback**

Answers on page 30.

WHAT DOES A ROBOT LOOK LIKE?

You might think a robot looks a little like a metal human – with a face, arms and legs. But robots can look all sorts of different ways depending on the job they do. Some might look like big boxes while some look like creepy crawlies. Factory robots don't usually look like anything else – they are just machinery designed to carry out their bit of work.

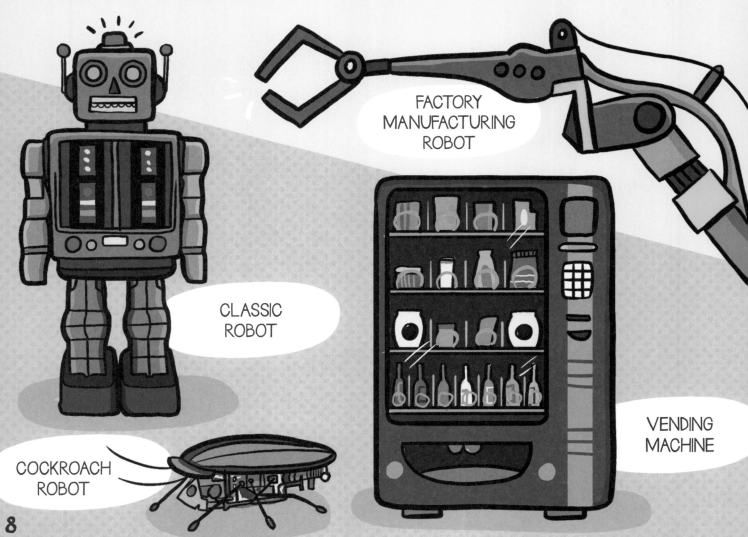

FACTORY MANUFACTURING ROBOT

CLASSIC ROBOT

VENDING MACHINE

COCKROACH ROBOT

What do you imagine a robot to look like?

Draw your robot here!

Things to consider:

- What job will your robot do?
- How will it sense its environment?
- How will it move?
- What will its body look like?
- Where will its power come from?

ROBOT BODIES

When designing how a robot should look, engineers consider how the robot will move, what size it should be, where it will need to go, and how quickly or smoothly it should move. Some robots look like humans because they are designed to do work that humans do, but engineers are just as likely to design robots that look like animals, or like nothing seen before!

JOBS

HELP POLLINATE FLOWERS

SCOUT FOR DANGER FOR THE U.S. ARMY

TRAVEL THROUGH SMALL GAPS TO FIND SURVIVORS OF EARTHQUAKES

TRAVEL THROUGH YOUR BODY TO DELIVER MEDICINE

CARRY PACKAGES ACROSS DIFFICULT MUD OR SNOW

Match these robots to the jobs they do.

ROBOTS

6 MM LONG

MILI -
A CURL OF SILICONE

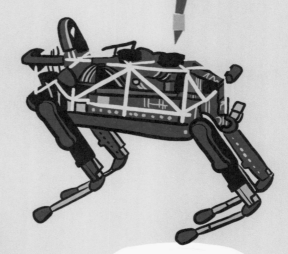

SPOT, THE
ROBOTIC DOG

COCKROACH
ROBOT

ROBOBEE

BIG DOG

These are all real
robots, though some of them
are still being developed.

BUILD A ROBOT

You can design a robot to do several jobs by
building in the right hardware to do each part of
the job. Robots don't have to look like people but
we often think they look friendlier if they do!

Turn this simple robot into
one that can make breakfast
by bolting on the most useful
attachments. Where would
each part go? Draw your
breakfast robot here!

oven
attachment

cutlery
fingers

kettle

spatula
attachment

fridge

oven
gloves

toaster

whisk
attachment

jam
squirter

Choose what to give this robot so it can help you with your homework!

pens and pencils

mini library

eraser

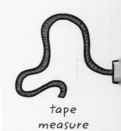

tape measure

calculator

stencils

ear attachment to translate other languages

speaker to repeat times tables

ROBOT JOBS

What robots can do is limited only by our imaginations and the technology we have available.

Here are some pieces of hardware that can be used in robotics to do particular jobs.

Buzzer
for making noise

Lever
for lifting and lowering

Movement sensor
to detect when something is moving nearby

Heating element
can get hot

Light
to see in the dark

Smoke sensor
to detect smoke in the air

Light sensor
to detect when it's getting dark

Temperature sensor
to detect when the temperature goes up or down

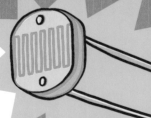

Imagine you are building a robot to do each of these jobs. Tick which of these pieces of hardware you would choose for each robot. The first has been done for you.

Hardware	Burglar alarm	Toaster	Glow-in-the-dark key ring	Fire alarm
Lever				
Movement sensor	✔			
Light sensor				
Temperature sensor				
Smoke sensor				
Light				
Buzzer	✔			
Heating element				

Can you think of another job a robot could do with any combination of these things? Draw or write about it here.

CIRCUITS

Robots are powered by electricity and when the power is switched on, electricity flows through wires so the robot can work. Electricity wires are arranged in a circuit. When the electric circuit is complete, electricity can flow through the wires and power the robot. If the circuit is not complete or is broken, the electricity cannot flow around the circuit and the robot won't work.

Electricity flows from the battery...

...continues in a circuit...

...and the electric circuit powers the light bulb!

This switch is open and has broken the circuit, so the circuit can't power the light bulb.

Which electricity circuit powers which robot? Complete each circuit by colouring each wire with a different coloured pen or pencil to find out what job each robot does. One robot has a broken circuit. Which piece of hardware will not work?

3:26

ROBOT MATERIALS

Robots can be made from all sorts of materials and engineers make sure they pick the right material for the job. Different materials have different qualities, which suit different needs of different robots. Because electricity can make heat, it's important that robot 'bodies' are heat and fire resistant. If a robot will travel in water, its electronics will need to be kept in waterproof material. If a robot is going to fly, it will need to be made of material that's light.

This table shows some typical properties of each of these materials. Use this information to help you choose a good material to build the bodies of each of these robots.

Write the best materials under each robot.

	light	easy to shape	won't snap	won't bend	won't set on fire	see-through	can be squeezed
ALUMINIUM	✔	✔	✔		✔		
STEEL			✔	✔	✔		
GLASS				✔	✔	✔	
PLEXIGLASS				✔	✔	✔	
WOOD		✔		✔			
RUBBER		✔	✔				✔
PLASTIC	✔	✔		✔			

18

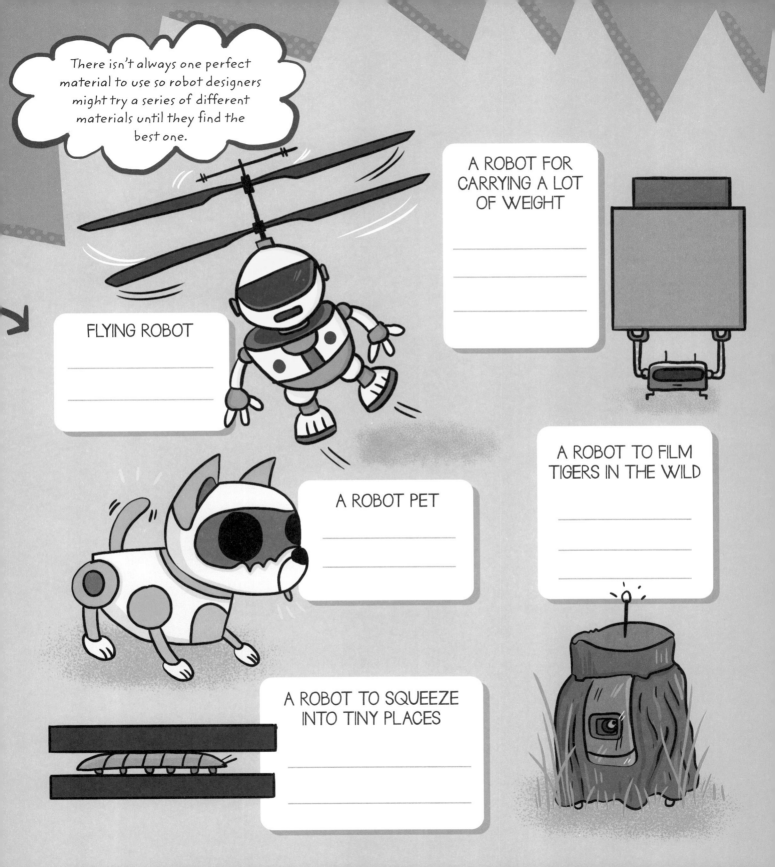

There isn't always one perfect material to use so robot designers might try a series of different materials until they find the best one.

A ROBOT FOR CARRYING A LOT OF WEIGHT

FLYING ROBOT

A ROBOT TO FILM TIGERS IN THE WILD

A ROBOT PET

A ROBOT TO SQUEEZE INTO TINY PLACES

COGS AND LEVERS

Some robots were invented even before electricity had been discovered. Leonardo da Vinci designed a mechanical robot 500 years ago, which could sit, stand, turn its head and move its arms.

The science of creating movement is called 'mechanics', and to make his robot move da Vinci used a combination of simple mechanics like cogs and levers – the same sort of mechanics that help a bicycle move.

Levers are like see-saws: if you press down at one end, the other end will move upwards. If the fulcrum is in the middle of the lever, the lever balances when the weight on each end is equal.

If the fulcrum is closer to one end, you can move a heavy weight by putting it on the shorter end and pushing down with less force on the longer end.

A cog is a wheel with teeth that fits into another wheel with teeth – so when you turn one wheel, the wheel slotted into it will also turn, but in the opposite direction. If two cogs working together are different sizes, the smaller one turns more often than the bigger one. The slower turning cog has more power than the smaller, faster one.

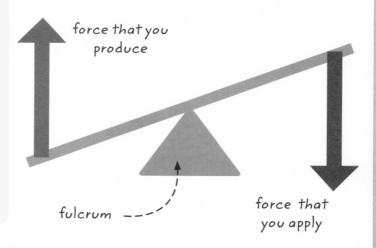

force that you produce

fulcrum

force that you apply

20

Mechanics can build machines by making cogs and levers work together. Using what you know about cogs and levers, work out which way each cog will turn and find out if the package at the end will end up at A or B.
The arrows on the first two cogs have been done for you.

Wire

B

A

WAREHOUSE WORK

Robots can do very complicated and precise work but even big jobs are made up of a combination of small jobs in a particular order.

THIS ROBOT CAN DO FOUR SIMPLE JOBS:

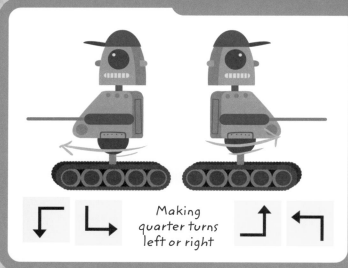

Making quarter turns left or right

Travelling

Lifting arms up and down

Tilting forwards and backwards

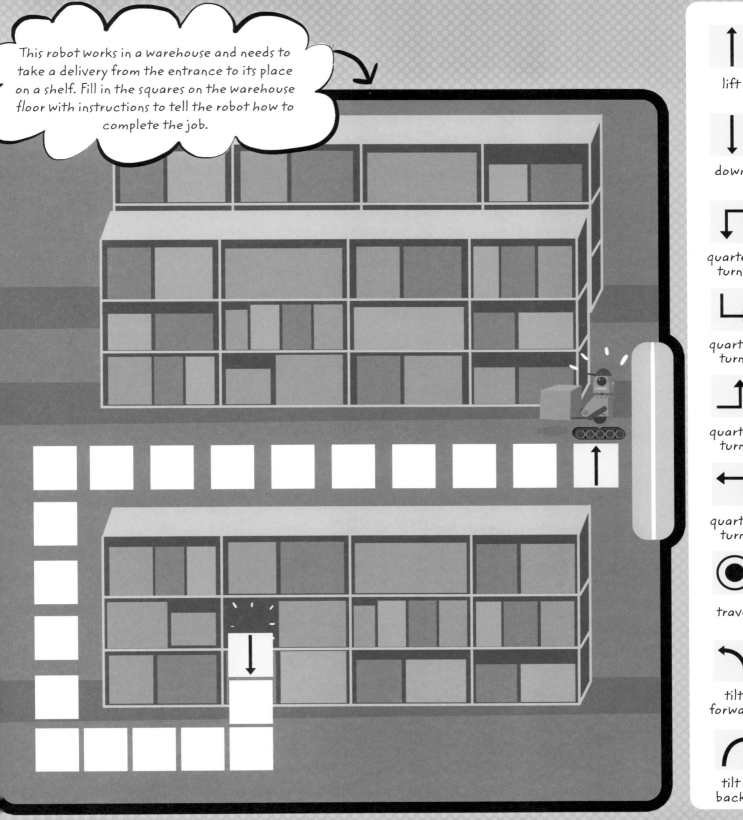

This robot works in a warehouse and needs to take a delivery from the entrance to its place on a shelf. Fill in the squares on the warehouse floor with instructions to tell the robot how to complete the job.

lift

down

quarter turn

quarter turn

quarter turn

quarter turn

travel

tilt forward

tilt back

READING CODE

Robots are programmed using code, which is a way of telling them a series of instructions to carry out. A robot's job is to turn the code into something useful.

Imagine you are a robot who has been given this code for colouring in a particular set of squares in this grid. Follow the instructions by colouring in each of the squares in this list of code and find out what the result is.

A: 3, 4, 5, 15, 16, 17

B: 2, 6, 14, 18

C: 1, 7, 13, 19

D: 1, 8, 12, 19

E: 1, 9, 11, 19

F: 1, 10, 19

G: 1, 19

H: 1, 6, 7, 13, 14, 19

I: 1, 6, 7, 13, 14, 19

J: 1, 19

K: 2, 9, 11, 18

L: 2, 10, 18

M: 3, 17

N: 4, 16

O: 5, 15

P: 6, 14

Q: 7, 13

R: 8, 12

S: 9, 11

T: 10

	1	2	3	4	5	6	7	8	9	10	11	12	13	14	15	16	17	18	19
A			■																
B																			
C																			
D																			
E																			
F																			
G																			
H																			
I																			
J																			
K																			
L																			
M																			
N																			
O																			
P																			
Q																			
R																			
S																			
T																			

And try this one too . . .

A: 9, 10, 11, 12

B: 8, 9, 12, 13

C: 8, 13

D: 8, 13

E: 5, 8, 9, 12, 13, 16

F: 5, 6, 9, 10, 11, 12, 15, 16

G: 6, 10, 11, 15

H: 6, 7, 10, 11, 13, 14, 15

I: 7, 8, 9, 10, 11, 12, 13

J: 10, 11

K: 10, 11

L: 10, 11

M: 9, 10, 11, 12

N: 8, 9, 12, 13

O: 8, 13

P: 8, 9, 12, 13

Q: 9, 10, 11, 12

R: 9, 11

S: 8, 9, 11, 12

T: 8, 12

U: 8, 12

V: 7, 8, 12, 13

	1	2	3	4	5	6	7	8	9	10	11	12	13	14	15	16	17	18	19
A																			
B																			
C																			
D																			
E																			
F																			
G																			
H																			
I																			
J																			
K																			
L																			
M																			
N																			
O																			
P																			
Q																			
R																			
S																			
T																			
U																			
V																			

WRITING CODE

Robots respond to code and engineers program robots by writing the code. The important thing to remember about writing code is that robots can only do what we program them to do. And they will only do things in the order the code has been written. So if you are writing code (or 'instructions') for a robot to bake a cake, it is a problem if the code tells the robot to put the cake tins into the oven before the mixture has been poured into the tins!

This robot needs to travel through this grid without stepping on a square that contains a banana skin. Write some code to lead the robot from start to finish without slipping up.

Step 1: Use a pencil to draw a path through the grid that avoids the bananas.

Step 2: Write a list of the steps the robot needs to take to be able to follow the path you have drawn.

The first three steps have been done for you.

1: forward 2 squares

2: turn right

3: forward 1 square

4: _____

5: _____

6: _____

7: _____

8: _____

9: _____

10: _____

11: _____

12: _____

13: _____

14: _____

15: _____

26

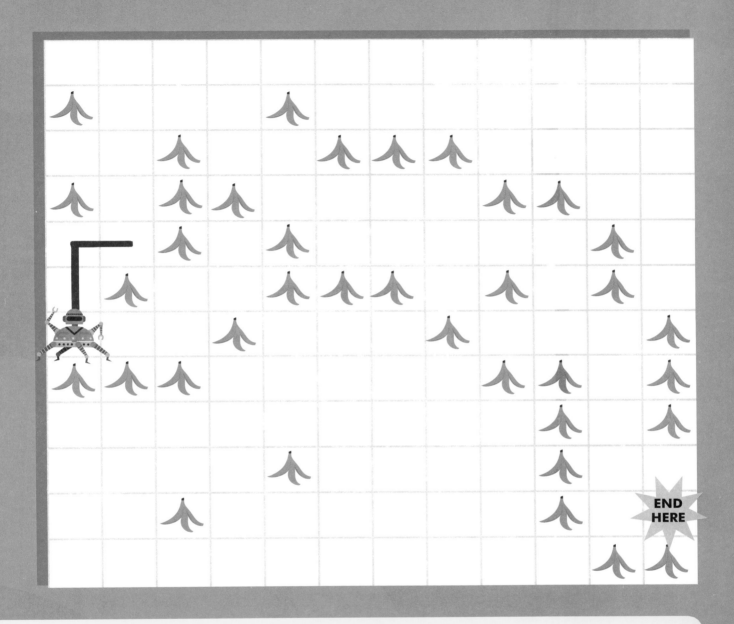

16: _____ 21: _____ 26: _____

17: _____ 22: _____ 27: _____

18: _____ 23: _____

19: _____ 24: _____

20: _____ 25: _____

FUTURE ROBOT

What jobs will the robots of the future do? Engineers have developed robots that can turn themselves into recycling when they have done their job, that can fool humans into thinking that they are talking to another human rather than a robot, and that can be powered and controlled by magnets rather than electricity. Exactly what the robots of the future could do is limited only by our human imaginations.

But there are some jobs that humans will never want to hand over to robots such as the more creative jobs or ones that are not dangerous.

Which of these jobs do you think could be done by a robot? Circle them in blue.
Which of these jobs do you think humans will want to still do in the future? Circle them in red.
Did you circle any of the jobs in both colours? Perhaps humans and robots will both want to do the same jobs!

journalist

football player

surgeon

teacher

builder

bus driver

baker

actor

illustrator

hairdresser

shop assistant

street cleaner

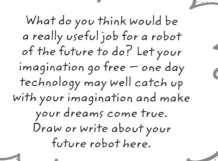

What do you think would be a really useful job for a robot of the future to do? Let your imagination go free — one day technology may well catch up with your imagination and make your dreams come true. Draw or write about your future robot here.

ANSWERS

pages 4-5 --->

TRUE	FALSE
Robots can dance — yes, if they are programmed to!	Robots are made of metal – a robot can be made of any material that suits its job!
Robots can play chess — yes, and in 2017 a robot even taught itself to play chess and beat the computer chess champion!	Robots have two arms and two legs – not necessarily!
Robots are used to diffuse bombs — yes, they have been used for more than forty years!	Microscopic robots can travel around your body to cure disease – not yet, but scientists are working on it!

pages 6-7 --->

```
d t h j d e l q s x y d e o h v p
y o n u p n t c r i l q g i u v e
k t i y t a s k u s e d i n e n a
c g d k c r u s l e e h w x g n n
a a e o c m i t o d a a e i r t u
b n a i g x e o u s t h s i t l t
d f s y j l t t e s v e h l f e a
e y w g o e u n c t d p l m v u i
e c v x s g s e r y i n e e o h l
f r s r i o p e s l o v u c l n p
h e t u r c v i o g l r u h c e o
i h p r o g r a m m i n g a n r w
c t j u r b c k s t i w n n l t e
d s y i s y f d s z h a a i o u r
a y i v o l c u j a m g o c e y c
s e l e c t r o n i c s c s i k j
g e t c u z y s e o j a v t f v a
```

pages 10-11 --->

30

pages 14-15

Hardware	Burglar alarm	Toaster	Glow-in-the-dark key ring	Fire alarm
Lever		✔		
Movement sensor	✔			
Light sensor			✔	
Temperature sensor				✔
Smoke sensor				✔
Light			✔	✔
Buzzer	✔			✔
Heating element		✔		

page 17

The fan will not work.

pages 18-19

aluminium because it's light, and plastic

any of the materials could work as the pet will be fairly small

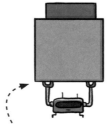

steel because it's strong and won't snap or bend, or wood because it is strong but lighter than steel

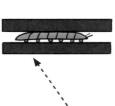

rubber because it is bendy

glass or plexiglass for the camera to film through, and wood to blend in with the surroundings

page 21

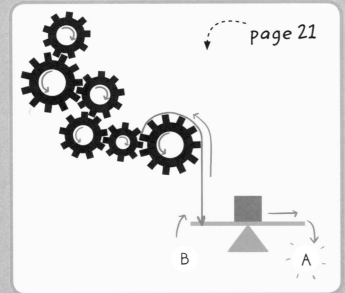

B   A

page 23

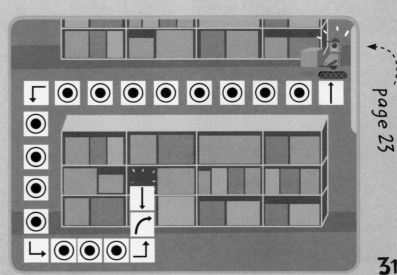

pages 24-25

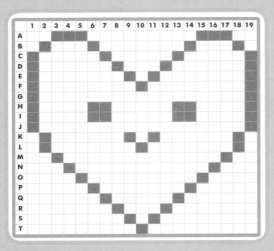

pages 28-29

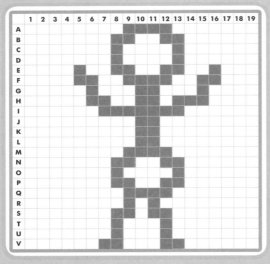

pages 26-27

1: forward 2 squares
2: turn right
3: forward 1 square
4: turn left
5: forward 3 squares
6: turn right
7: forward 2 squares
8: turn right
9: forward 1 square
10: turn left
11: forward 1 square
12: turn right
13: forward 1 square
14: turn left
15: forward 3 squares
16: turn right
17: forward 1 square
18: turn left
19: forward 2 squares
20: turn right
21: forward 2 squares
22: turn left
23: forward 1 square
24: turn right
25: forward 4 squares
26: turn left
27: forward 1 square

JOBS ROBOTS COULD DO

Surgeon — robots will be able to do some operations.

Teacher — people are already learning languages and other skills without humans teaching them, but humans will always be better at empathising with pupils and understanding what they need.

Bus driver — driverless cars are already being developed and some trains have been travelling without a driver for a long time.

Street cleaner - street cleaning vehicles are currently driven by people but might one day be programmed to run automatically.

Shop assistant — robots can do simple shop assistant jobs but humans are better at giving opinions and answers to customer questions.

Baker — some things, such as bread and cakes made in factories, are easily made by robots, but it's harder for robots to make up beautiful decorations and designs unless a human programs them.

Builder — robots will be able to put together whole houses from pre-made parts.